AN ELEGANCE OF GANNETS

€2.00 from the sale of this book will be donated to BirdWatchIreland

An Elegance of Gannets

Eithne Cavanagh

Photographs by Colum Clarke

Swan Press

Swan Press
32 Joy Street
Dublin 4

Copyright © with author, 2009

ISBN 978-0-9560496-2-9

Photographs by Colum Clarke
Cover photo: Gannet. Unst, Shetland Islands

Design & Layout by M & J Graphics, Dublin
Printed by Future Print, Dublin

By the same author
Bone and Petals, Swan Press 2001

Godwit, Kilcoole, Co. Wicklow.

ACKNOWLEDGEMENTS

Acknowledgements are due to the following publications:
The Stinging Fly, 100 Poems of GB and Ireland, ed: James
Knox Whittet, RI*POSTE, Between the Circus and the Sewer,
Cutting Teeth, Extended Wings* nos. 2 & 5, *Disarm,
Brobdingnagian Times, Studies, Boyne Berries, Connaught
Telegraph, Seeing the Wood and the Trees,* eds Rosemarie
Rowley & John Haughton, *Scríobh Anthology.* ed. Aoife
Flynn.

Some of these poems have been broadcast on radio.

I would like to thank Christine Broe, Susan Flynn,
Mary Guckian and Mary Shine for their encouragement.
I would also like to thank the management and staff
at Tyrone Gutherie Centre, Annaghmakerrig,
also Rathmines Writers.

For Colum

Sun silvered Shannon
swan glides majestically
river bends our journey

Contents

Discovery

Lost in a swirl of words
blinded by newness of light
I smell mudcolours.

You are a new country
deep craters, unplumbed seas,
a place of old growth, new shoots.

I am an otter, musk–damp
my sinuous pelt gleams
starbright by the river bank.

You strew poems along the water,
my strong jaws clamp nourishment
silver as fish.

The Fuchsias of Sherkin

If God is a dancer She'll shed tears
of laughter come August
when the hedges are red with tiny ballerinas,
petal skirted, and the wind chimes their name
*Deora Dé, Deora Dé.**

The soft brush of leaves cool my arm
and summery earth yields a rich musk.
I delicately nip flowers,
tasting again their secret nectar
guilty sweetness exploding my mouth.

Drunk on honeyed sips, I pirouctte
the petal'd path. God sings their name
Deora Dé, Deora Dé.

Puffins, Fair Isle, Scotland.

For Patrick and William*

Your gravestone surprises me high on Skellig rock
at the doorway to the sanctum damp with mist.

The lighthouse keeper carried your tiny coffins
over the Saddle of Christ

climbing grief's footfalls to bury two small sons
in the monks' old garden graced by jagged boulders.

We don't know how you died
but pray you laughed at puffins, had tickling games

with gannet feathers, hide-and-seek in lighthouse crannies,
beacon glowing, your stone-safe haven.

Exploring the Beehive huts I cannot now connect
with prayerful chant of monks, but fancy that I hear

your baby tones gurgling, laughing, crying,
cherub souls lingering on the upwinds.

Skellig Rock Daguerreotype

It is their kingdom, this sanctuary rock
of *cailleach** fingers scraping Atlantic sky.
Here gannets land and take off from a ledge
flat as an open palm and soft with feathers.

Her boat lightly dances the ring of foam.
A silvery rise of vapour salt-stings her face,
seabird symphony counterpoints the wind.
Feet firm on deck she primes her camera,

avid to record this communion with The Skellig,
and prove her oneness with such a sacred place.
The viewfinder frames an arch of rock,
keyhole to eternal ocean, but her film has run out.

Later, the untaken snapshot burns mercurial
in the darkroom of her own remembering.

The Search

Yesterday under cerulean sky
your house sunshone a safe smile.
Carmine lipped geraniums
blushed a whitewashed wall.

Today Atlantic rainclouds
crash above Inis Meáin
diluting the Idyll.

Silent, I trace the torrent
through limestone grikes
deep into cave rib.
Somewhere here your treasure
which I crave.

Stumbling on ice age boulders
I pick-axe the flinty seams
custodians of your soul
which if I find, unaided,
you promise will be mine.

Waiting in Kilronan

Not young, not old
your wise and childlike eyes
seek comfort in your glass
cradling whiskey'ed firelight.

An ancient sun ignites
primeval rocks and you recall
two women of the North wind
blue gowns edged with gold.
They did not touch your cheek
but vanished as you reached
to them across the slippery
moon-wet crags.

Atlantic tides have nibbled cliffs,
your neighbours' nets weigh rich
with salmon, pollock, mackerel.
Kelp enriches hungry soil,
men have drowned
and women encircle birth.
Ashes shift, pale moon shavings,
your glass now emptied
of flickering reflection.

The women of the North Wind
they never touched your face,
you dream of their return
refill your *deoch* content to wait.

Inishbofin Sheep Shearing

"Three sheep a day
is enough for a woman."
half-moon metal
gleaming in your hand.

Two days ago
you almost lost your man
- a coronary while fishing.
Now your keen eye regards
three ewes, legs trussed,
twitching on green plastic.

We try to help.
Eyeball to eyeball with a sheep
for the first time
our city hands feel
rough ridges of horn
and delicacy of ankle,
as we hold her steady
for your expert cut.

Free at last, bald, vulnerable,
she stumbles on dainty hooves
looking prehistoric.
Her twin lambs bleat, hesitate,
then rush for milk.

Anointed with oily fleece
we prepare to handle
two more ewes
our quota for today.

The Walk

Pewter sky, seabirds at rest
white stones smoothed by Atlantic movement,
gargoyle driftwood, rusted metal,
a child's sandal lost one summer day.

The lone walker holds a stone,
time frozen egg,
feels its roundness
marvels at its whiteness.
Tongue on stone, salt.

The walker throws the stone
in a great arching circle to the waves,
throws another and another, yet another
madly trying to empty cobble beach
into the ocean.

Easterly, a crescent glows,
pale light touches ragged wave
lapping over moonwhite shore
and Atlantic grinds forever.

Pirate Queen

Pirate Queen

Red fuchsia bells bedeck your rocks,
honeysuckle still entwines, fragrant,
into every crevice of Clare island.

A barefoot child you ran the hills
to play around pre-Christian tombs;
hide and seek, three legged races.

Jeering at your boyish haircut
they called you Bald Grace
when you joined your father's ships

to learn the noble trade of pirating
the skills of navigation, plunder,
on roll and pitch of creamy foam.

Gunnel-full of spice and glass,
Spanish wine and fabrics rich,
you skippered the finest galleys

swifter than the corsair of the Turks
disabled by your own blunderbuss
and you a day from childbed.

A woman of power and consequence
unbowed by the Tudor Queen
she of the ruffs, bejewelled gowns.

Your saffron cloak and silver torc
cut quite a dash as you strode
through her pomandered halls

spraying the air with salt and brine.
You silence with a flashing glance
effete court titterings at your garb.

Perhaps you and Liz did sup
chit-chatting about envoys, politicians,
in a sort of women's alliance

(or discussed the fashions of the day
admiring each other's style
and swapping combs of tortoiseshell).

Both of you commanded men
humble kerne, swashbuckled prince
vassals all, within your liege.

Yes, Gránuaile, I walk your island
and do seek the honey-holes of bees
which you surely would have known.

Tonight your castle, a moonlit beacon,
guides a phantom ship, sails full,
to the shore where I await your landing

and offer you a goblet overflowing
with fuchsia-pollen mead.

St. Columcille's Well

Watch where you put your feet
here on slithery rocks
as wet ferns slap your legs.
This lushness hides a cairn,
crescent-shaped, generations built,
its moon-bleached arms embrace
and guard the holy well.

They've been here before you
the prayerful ones,
the cynics, the hopeful
and sensation seekers.
Leave your offering among theirs.
Sip the peaty water
and say a little prayer.
Touch the beads that hang
around the neck of weathered saint
- someone's sacred plea.

Stand on a high stone
shout or whisper
your intention to the wind
while black faced sheep graze
in snug and woolly circle,
their rhythmic chewing like soft
response to ancient litany.

Shag and Cormorant, Sandycove, Co. Dublin.

Slieve League Observes a Vertiginous Climber

I flaunt my steep cliffs frilled above the sea
and dip my toes in waves that glint like prisms
of jagged glass. Wearing cerise shirt, she
eyes the narrow path, a precarious ribbon
called 'One Man's Pass' with jittery suspicion.
Her stomach churns, she wishes she could glide
to my stone cap, her self-appointed mission.
Cerise bosom all puffed up with pride
she skitters, scrambles, conquers my craggy flanks.
With mucky knees and soil beneath her nails
she spies blue Nephin miraged in the distance,
Ben Bulben's flat head peeps through dizzy haze.

I twitch my heather skirts, savouring the fun,
vertigo compels her to descend upon her bum.

Tory Island Images

Tory Island Images

1   The Artist's Hut

In the unbelievably blue sphere
of sea and sky she peels an orange

and separates the segments.
Juice splashes the saffron-lichened rocks.

On tiptoe at the artist's hut
she sees a moth trapped behind grimy glass,

a tub of Polyfilla, empty coathangers,
pillows, their ticking all torn.

Linseed oil, paintbrushes stiff with disuse
seem to wait for his ghost

to sweep across canvas
capture the vastness, release the moth.

2   *Legends*

Etching the skyline Errigal, Muckish,
are robed in bleached denim haze.

Her world is fragrant with ozone and pollen
faded seapinks flutter papery shells.

Chough, cormorants and gulls wheel
by crags unchanged since one-eyed Balor

imprisoned his daughter for daring to love,
or since Columcille blessed a handful of clay.

She finishes her orange, zest scenting the blue
with hints of Morocco, 'African Mariners',

pirates of legend and poem.
she dreams ships laden with gold, spices and silk,

a moth wings past her head
like a spirit following flight to infinity.

3   *The Céilí*

At midnight or so the music starts,
Patsy Dan's accordion sets toes a-twitching.

The Waves of Tory and the Stack of Barley
undulate around the hall.

A sixteen-hand reel gains momentum,
its rhythms spiralling into time,

the human whirligig spins faster, faster
while a bodhran speeds up the beat.

Music spilling out over her head,
she dances towards the lighthouse beam

to the fringe of the world where the artist's hut
stands black and angled against the moon.

Bearings

We think we know these hills,
can throw away the map
needless at the peak.
My hair tangled and wet
I swivel you around to read
the tracery of your face,
a chart I've used for years.
Each line is known to me
yet I can no longer decipher
the markings of new strata.

We contour a steep place
to navigate an easier path.
From the summit we survey
our travelled landscape
and head for open ground.
Checking the legend
we hope to bypass hazards,
but the map has faded
flaky like old parchment
our bearings all awry.

Razorbill Sanctuary

It takes patience to watch a hatching.
By the lighthouse we hold our stance of silence
as if mere breathing would disturb
the razorbills' protective circle.

The powerful lens magnifies our quest
- a fluffy chick
snug in his world on rain slicked Rathlin cliff.

I stretch a wind-salted hand
half expecting transmission through the lens
half expecting to feel the soft throb breaking into light.

My focus sharpens.
A raucous symphony curves the air,
this chick becomes my universe,
rocks forever sanctuary.

Razorbills, Rathlin Island, Co. Antrim.

Fridarey*

To knit you an island
I will first take some mauve heather,

ochre lichen and fluffy white bog cotton.
I'll thread these with silverseasparkle.

My circular needle will shape yarn
woven from granite and peat

into zigzagging chevrons –
the wing patterns of bonxies*.

I will brave the bomb-diving
squadrons of skua,

ignore their hiss and their spit
just to knit you an island.

For a bit of frivolity I'll fashion
a few puffins to put round the edges.

But how can I knit
the calling, the murling, the whirring,

the orchestra of wind and the birds
which will music your island?

I will go to the rim of the blue
unravel some clouds

and purl shreds of consciousness
into the nest of things.

At Hermaness

Myth and seabirds meet
at this northern tip of Unst,
here two giants, for love of a mermaid
hurled rocks across the Burra Firth.

Lighthouse at Muckle Flugga in my sights
I walk the spongy bog,
in the sky an elegance of gannets
haughty as if a make-up artist extraordinaire

had shadowed their eyes
with smoky kohl
black-lined each beak,
then sprayed faintest yellow on their heads.

No mermaid I,
no giants compete for my hand,
the twin headlands of Hermaness
and Saxa Vord become my kingdom for today.

I fuse into pinkgrey of gneiss and granite
the contents of my mind flown out,
out far beyond the giants' rocks.

Voices from the Osberg

Voices from the Osberg*

Queen Asa speaks

I did not ask that she be killed, buried along with me.
Though a high-born woman I had no choice,
a chamber hung with tapestries would have been enough.

Nor did I want twelve fine horses slaughtered
in ceremonial pomp just to satisfy the gods
and prove how powerful is my husband.

Here in our burial ship deep within its mound of clay
they placed food for our passage, two oxen,
fresh dough, wild apples, blueberries and herbs.

My time had come to lie within the ribs, the salt ribs,
sink back into the earth, escape from pain.
But she was young, sinewy, would have given birth.

Feel the softness of my shoes, calf's hide
specially crafted to caress my painful foot.
Look, see how worn the scuffed right shoe is.

I remember how she, my maid, bathed these feet
in warm goat's milk and leather-stitched my jerkin
into the long sun of summer nights.

She groomed my hair with a carved elk-bone comb,
Oh! That welcome sharpness on my scalp.
She dressed it the way I like it, just a little to the side.

They buried me in a fine wool gown, a shawl of silk.
They left milk pails and buckets here, a loom,
needles, and some cloth, my women's work.

But I will continue with the weaving
I'll work the spindle, the niddy-noddies as I learned
to do in childhood while my nursemaid wove for me

tapestries and sagas of horses, carts and gods,
and all familiar things,
like fresh dough, wild apples, blueberries and herbs.

The Maid speaks

They ripped me from my lover's bed
snug with softened skins
warm with the imprint of our bodies.

I bit and fought and kicked for life.
I served her well and was cursed to die with her.
She could have ordered that I live,

but no, Her Ladyship must have the slave to hand.
I should see years of winter snow,
summer light on birches, my children's growth.

How gently I washed her feet in fresh goat's milk,
finely stitched her gowns
brought her gifts of wild red apples,

gave sympathy, dressed her scraggy hair,
(though I did enjoy being rough
with that fancy comb she liked so much).

They buried her in rich fabrics sewn by me.
I will not attend her now, knead the dough,
stir the cooking pot or carry pails of milk.

Let her rot with the ghosts of slaughtered horses
in the dank chamber of this stinking ship
where foetid earth presses on my head.

The loom is here, I will weave a belt for him.
a wide belt of many colours,
dyed with lichens, moss and mountain grasses.

I want to crunch the sweet flesh of wild apples
lazily suck the juice of blueberries
and lie with him again crushing the summer herbs.

Arctic Skua, Hermaness, Unst, Shetland, Scotland.

The Shape of Trees

Fine rain opaques the forest.
She moves into the green light
sandals squelching
raindribbles cool her neck.

Head stretched backwards
she admires the gothic arch
of high birches.
White sky stings her eyes.

No one can find her here.

Striding through high ferns
she knows that she is:
prouder than a tigress
more timid than a fawn
craftier than a fox.

Motionless, she welcomes
the heavy splash of rain
submitting to a new baptism.

Swinburne's Grave

An innocence of snowdrops brightens
the graveyard of St. Boniface,
white bells nod around the tomb
where lies the satyrs' Laureate.

Between moss and rock, discrete,
the old church nestles
in February chill, revealing nothing
of Charles Algernon's excesses.

Further down the chalky chine *
sea waves frolic in mad exuberance
a breezy tango – licentious dance
for 'that demonic boy' of Wight.

By the Wind

The seal-song filled air
saltsprays my face.
I offer you a 'By the Wind Sailor'.*

A tiny jellyfish! You scoff
at such a gift
lying glutinous in your hand.

We examine the inky cobweb veins
like the labyrinth of paths
we've walked, climbed, stumbled.

The transparent frilled sail
looks too fragile to voyage
the tidal surges of our lives.

You sail your own course
tacking, windrunning but always
parallel to the slippery rocks

and I watch the horizon from a shell
watching for your return
to the shores of our seal-song.

Seal Song, Bardsey Island

Somewhere here Merlin's resting place.
I seek his cave, his house of glass.

Wind buffets my ears and I am lured
to the edge of land, towards music
in low toned flutes.

Smudging the dove-soft horizon
the rocks sheen damply,
dark seaweed drapes and tangles

heaving with languid movement
of mottled pewter bodies, ebony playfulness.

Lithe with sinewy writhings
the cove takes on enchantment,
a perfect auditorium for seal-song.

Whiskered faces twitch, staring, curious,
calm in ownership of their bay,
proprietors of this island.

No need here for charms, wands
or incantations, their song fills me

with an almost gracious sense
of welcome to their pearly crescent.

Saltee Island

May has flung wild fistfuls
of bluebells azuring the leeward slope.
On the wilder edge rocks glisten ochre
and palest silver.

Here, gannets glide past a high sun,
stiff wingspan filtering a light
whiter than fine organdie
veiling the muscle of their bullet-flight.

I almost feel the silky warmth
of their yellow heads.

You stroke my face with a feather
later saved between the pages
of my bird book. I pick a Sea Campion
to press its papery bloom,

but falter at the sappy stem
of bluebell bowed in a breeze
whispery as the sigh of vespers
just before the evening ferry sails.

Sands

A saffron-robed monk taps coloured sand
through copper funnel, tracing a template
in the slow, silent creation of a mandala.

The sand at Arklow is just right, tight-packed
and damp enough to shape a turret or a moat.
Children on the beach dig their own circle.

They decorate their castle
with shells, pebbles, seapinks, driftwood.
Later, the night sea gushes through the moat.

Each tidelap softens the outline
leaving no trace of childlike footprint.
No piping shouts linger on the air.

Flowerheads contain the stillness.
A resonance of holy chant trembles incense smoke,
while monks sweep up the blue

the green, the red and yellow grains
of life's impermanence which they carry
in procession to the nearest river.

The ocean ripple-sculpts a children's castle.
Tibetan temple bells chime beside the Liffey

and the seabirds' mantra never ceases.

Wavemusic

Frozen irons, my feet imprint the sand.
Shallow ripples shear my ankles,
shivering I delay to meet you at a deeper depth.

Earlier you admired my new black swimsuit
(Dunne's £9.99), decorous, straightcut at thigh
and draped at bust.

You declared a one-piece to be the more alluring.
Not caring about the honesty of your preference
I crest the swell to join you.

Soft as sunwarmed oil, the sea envelops us;
we splash and frolic
believing ourselves sinuous as seals.

Later, on vacant beach you pour sandkisses
into a curled shell
and wavemusic throbs our senses.

Magenta Sea

Years I have plunged deep
seeking pearls, but the seabed
yielded only empty shells.

One last time, I climb back
on our boat clinging
to the frayed rope,
its roughness burns my palms.

With a swift filleting slash
I unsplice our moorings
and cast myself adrift.

Salt water stings my wound,
heals and cleanses
as I prow strongly
into the magenta sea.

A Certain Light

There is a certain light of a May evening
which ambers the conifers' tall trunks.

There is a moment of life and stillness
in the beechwood just before the birds
get busy with their night time bustlings.

Here in the silence at the corner of the forest
I am embraced by that wooded Shishkin* landscape
which you loved.

It is here I taste again your presence
weightless on these broken twigs, my bones,
and dare to hope that I can now begin to travel on,

alone.

Waiting for a Kingfisher

A rowan tree scant shelter from the rain,
we hoped to see a kingfisher in flight
arrowing honeysuckle's fragrant chain,

and wondered if that bird would ever deign
to flaunt his jewels in order to delight
us huddling in scant shelter from the rain.

We began to feel our wait might be in vain,
picked blackberries fat with purple light,
brambling through the golden chain.

Across the riverbank pale-feathered crane
with one imperial flounce of plumage bright,
showed no need to shelter from the rain.

This dancing bird outdid Fonteyne.
With balletic leap of unbelievable height
he rose above the honeysuckle chain.

We waited, the kingfisher never came.
Our consolation prize - that single flash of white.
A rowan tree scant shelter from the rain
we lingered, tangled in a fragrant chain.

Before Thunder

Lush green trees
droop heavily,
weighed by summer's rain.
Full-blown roses musk the air.
A lazy wasp inspects each rose.
The stillness oppresses.
Only the elusive now exists.

The moment has passed
lazily like the wasp
to another now,
and yet another,
into an explosive
thunder
to eternity.

Conversation with a Corncrake

Conversation with a Corncrake

I heard you in wheatfields
when summers were real.
In the blue of night you rasped your call
unstilling the velvet heat.

We would nest in meadows of long grass
yellow irises or forget-me-nots bursting with pollen,
lush with insects.

I knew your sound and thought it friendly,
warm as the sun on a haycock
or newly laid eggs in the chicken coop.

We had peace in scything season.
the farmer's tread across the field
gave time to run for cover with our crakelings.

Long sunny days of playtime, stretching the game
until sunbeams faded on the wall of the shed
and crows were settling, you hid from me.

When they mowed hayfields with horses
the clatter of harness, glint of metal
was warning enough.

Wanting a glimpse of your speckled head
I looked for you in meadows,
played your 'crex-crex' game of hide-and-go-seek.

No, you never could find us
our nest snug in a jungle of loosestrife,
grassysmells, where we used to feel safe.

I loved the haysweetness of air
when mowing machines cut golden swathes
and larks swooped the white heat of sky.

Those tractors really did us in
spinning around the field, unmerciful,
smashing our nests, slicing our fledglings.

And then you were gone, on chestnut wings
again, to Africa's ochre plains
your cup of a nest crushed among stubble.

Fewer of us each year, we fly South
returning in spring
bound to our eternal life cycle.

Frozen Moment, Newgrange

*Luí liom mo dhilis**
The clear notes of an old slow air
rise from his tin whistle,
pure crystal in the iciness
of this corbelled chamber.
Quietly we contemplate spirals
tooled on ungiving rock.

Muffled in our scarves and gloves
we file the narrow passage,
emerge to light, where snow
fine as muslin lies filmy
over the nearby fields and hills
caressed by the old pale sun

...and his requiem for ancient souls
still echoes.

A New Year Sky

Across the unwritten sky
pale and clean as a fresh page
one swan appears
neck stretched in flight.

This white sculpted shape
of grace must have flown
from the hand
of some Italian stuccoist.

In wintry Drumsna
gale-bent Shannon grasses underfoot,
we look skyward, and wonder
where the swan is headed

- perhaps to join her flock
at some Connemara lake
or Hy Brasil or even Tir na nÓg,
a queenly odyssey to another world.

Our swan has disappeared now.
The sky bears no trace of silverchain
but her image sharply bones
into your soul and mine.

Notes

Fuchsias of Sherkin page 12
Deora Dé, God's tears, Irish for fuchsia.

For Patrick and William page 14
Patrick aged 2 died December 1868 and William aged 4 died March 1869. Both were sons of Skellig Rock Lighthouse keeper W. Callaghan.

Skellig Rock Daguerreotype page 15
Cailleach - witch.

Tory Island Images page 28
Artist Derek Hill 1916–2000 was the forerunner of the Tory school of naïve painting.

Fridarey page 34
Fridarey, Old Norse name for Fair Isle.
Bonxie, local name for the Great Skua.

Voices from the Osberg page 38
Osberg, a Viking burial ship discovered in Norway. It was usual to bury nobility with servants and food.

Niddy noddy page 39
A tool to make skeins from yarn.

Swinburne's Grave page 43
Chine, chalk cliffs found south England.

By the Wind page 44
By the Wind Sailor – Vela Vela a small jellyfish.

A Certain Light Page 50
Ivan Shishkin, 1832-1898. Russian landscape artist.

Frozen Moment, Newgrange page 56
Luí liom mo Dhílis, lie with me my loved one.

Fast as leaping trout
electric blue strikes river
kingfisher flashes

Kingfisher, Dargle River, Bray, Co. Wicklow.

Locations of Islands

1   Sherkin Island, West Cork

2   Skellig Rock, Co. Kerry

3   Skellig Michael, Co. Kerry

4   Inis Meáin, Aran Islands, Co. Galway

5   Inishmore, Aran Islands, Co Galway

6   Inishbofin, Co. Galway

7   Clare Island, Clew Bay, Co. Mayo

8   Tory Island, Co. Donegal

9   Rathlin Island, Co. Antrim

10   Fair Isle, Scotland

11   Unst, Shetland Islands, Scotland

12   Isle of Wight, England

13   Bardsey Island, Wales

14   Saltee Island, Co. Wexford